POINTS OF VIEW

Should Kids Go to PROTESTS?

By Amy B. Rogers

KidHaven PUBLISHING

Published in 2025 by
KidHaven Publishing, an Imprint of Greenhaven Publishing, LLC
2544 Clinton St.
Buffalo, NY 14224

Designer: Deanna Lepovich
Editor: Katie Kawa

Photo credits: Cover Ground Picture/Shutterstock.com; p. 5 (main) 1000 Words/Shutterstock.com; p. 5 (inset) 19bProduction/Shutterstock.com; p. 7 MikeDotta/Shutterstock.com; p. 9 (main) Sheila Fitzgerald/Shutterstock.com; p. 9 (inset) Ben Gingell/Shutterstock.com; p. 11 Cory Seamer/Shutterstock.com; p. 13 VDB Photos/Shutterstock.com; p. 15 lev radin/Shutterstock.com; p. 17 Dikushin Dmitry/Shutterstock.com; p. 19 Heartwood Films/Shutterstock.com; p. 21 (notepad) ESB Professional/Shutterstock.com; p. 21 (markers) Kucher Serhii/Shutterstock.com; p. 21 (photo frame) FARBAI/iStock/Thinkstock; p. 21 (inset, left) Ink Drop/Shutterstock.com; p. 21 (inset, right) Rawpixel.com/Shutterstock.com.

Library of Congress Cataloging-in-Publication Data

Names: Rogers, Amy B., author.
Title: Should kids go to protests? / Amy B. Rogers.
Description: Buffalo, New York : KidHaven Publishing, [2025] | Series: Points of view | Includes index.
Identifiers: LCCN 2023055200 | ISBN 9781534547681 (library binding) | ISBN 9781534547674 (paperback) | ISBN 9781534547698 (ebook)
Subjects: LCSH: Protest movements–Juvenile literature.
Classification: LCC HM883 .R64 2025 | DDC 303.48/40835–dc23/eng/20240129
LC record available at https://lccn.loc.gov/2023055200

Printed in the United States of America

CONTENTS

Calling for CHANGE

You're never too young to make your voice heard! People have found many ways to speak out about problems in the world and call for change. One important way people do this is through protests—gatherings where people come together to show they don't like something or want something to change.

Young people can often be seen at protests—and sometimes they even lead them. Some people think this is a good way to teach kids about active citizenship. Others, though, think kids should be kept away from protests. Keep reading to learn more about this **debate**!

It's important to form your own opinion about issues that **affect** you, such as this one. Do you think kids should go to protests? Before you answer, let's learn the facts about this issue and break down both sides of the debate.

Know the Facts!

The First Amendment to the U.S. Constitution **protects** citizens' rights to free speech, to gather peacefully, and to ask the government to fix things they feel are wrong. This amendment, or change, to the Constitution is part of a group of 10 amendments called the Bill of Rights.

Kids Make a DIFFERENCE

Young people have been at the front of many important protest movements throughout history. This includes the civil rights movement, which was a movement that called attention to the **racism**, inequality, and injustice faced by Black Americans. In May 1963, more than 1,000 young people in Birmingham, Alabama, skipped school to march against racism in what's sometimes called the Children's Crusade.

Protesting is important, but it's not always safe. Many young people who took part in the Children's Crusade were taken to jail. Some were sprayed with fire hoses and had to face dangerous, or unsafe, police dogs.

One of the biggest issues young people care about today is **climate change**. Fridays for Future, which is a worldwide protest movement dealing with this issue, was started by Greta Thunberg, who's shown here. She and other young people have planned many school strikes, in which students skip school to call attention to the dangers of climate change.

Know the Facts!

In 2018, school walkouts were held to call attention to problem of gun **violence** in the United States, especially in schools. Young people walked out of their classes to protest what they saw as a lack of concern, or worry, about their safety from the people in charge of making laws about guns.

Everyone Is AFFECTED

Many kids today are affected by racism, gun violence, and **intolerance**. This is one big reason why many people support kids going to—and leading—protests. Adults aren't the only ones who are affected by problems in the world around them. Kids are affected by them, too, so they should get to fight for a better world the same way adults do.

Kids are also the ones who are going to have to deal with these problems in the future. This is a big reason why kids are the ones leading the fight against climate change.

Know the Facts!

The Fridays for Future movement started in Stockholm, Sweden, in 2018 but has spread to more than 7,500 cities around the world.

Many people believe if kids are old enough to be dealing with problems such as gun violence, then they're old enough to have opinions about these problems and to call for changes in how we deal with them.

Too YOUNG?

In some cases, kids decide for themselves that they want to attend a protest because they care about an issue. In other cases, parents or guardians take their kids to a protest about an issue they care about. It's important for kids to always attend a protest with a trusted adult, but some people believe adults shouldn't take kids to protests, especially if their child didn't ask to go.

These people believe taking a child to a protest keeps them from forming their own opinions about an issue. Instead, they argue that child will grow up believing only what they're surrounded by.

Some people argue that kids shouldn't go to protests until they're old enough to form their own opinions about current events. They worry that attending protests from a young age keeps kids from seeing other sides of a debate and learning to think for themselves.

Know the Facts!

According to a study done by a group called the Pew Research Center, more than 80 percent of teenagers share the same **political** beliefs as at least one of their parents.

Raising Active CITIZENS

Many adults who bring their children to protests argue that they're not trying to force their views of the world on their kids. Instead, they want to show their kids how important it is to use their voices to speak out about any issue that's important to them.

Attending a protest also gives kids a chance to learn more about their rights and freedoms. Protests are examples of active citizenship in action, and many adults hope their kids will grow up to be active citizens—people who work to make a difference in their community and their country.

Some people think taking kids to a protest is a good way to teach them about civics, which deals with the rights and **responsibilities** of citizens.

Know the Facts!

Children have rights too. The United Nations Convention on the Rights of the Child is an agreement signed by 196 countries that lists the rights of children around the world. According to this agreement, children have the right to freely share their thoughts and feelings and to gather in groups to peacefully protest.

Sometimes

SCARY

Protests can teach children good lessons about civics. However, some people argue that it can also teach children about upsetting things. Protesters sometimes use bad words or other kinds of hurtful language, and some adults think children shouldn't be **exposed** to that.

In addition, there are sometimes counterprotesters at a protest. These are people who hold the opposite point of view. Protesters and counterprotesters might yell hurtful things at each other, and this could make kids scared or upset. In general, protests are often loud, crowded events, and this can often make kids—and even adults—feel anxious.

Know the Facts!

Millions of kids in the United States live with anxiety. This is a mental health condition—a condition that affects that mind. It is marked by strong feelings of worry and fear about what might happen.

People at protests and counterprotests often have strong feelings. This can lead to yelling, arguing, and sometimes even violence. This can be scary for kids, especially for kids who already deal with anxiety.

Fighting FEAR

Some people argue that attending protests might cause anxiety. Others, however, believe the opposite is true. They argue that taking part in a protest can be a good way to help kids who feel anxious about scary things that are happening in the world.

For example, kids might feel anxious about gun violence after hearing about it on the news or doing safety drills at school. One way to help them might be to take them to a protest where people are calling for an end to gun violence. This shows them that people are fighting to keep them safe.

Know the Facts!

A 2021 study of young people in 10 countries, including the United States, showed that 95 percent of them were worried about climate change.

When kids hear about big problems, such as climate change, gun violence, or war, they can sometimes feel like there's nothing they can do about them. Some people believe taking kids to a protest can help them feel more hopeful about the future and sure of their ability to help make the world a better place.

Not Always SAFE

Going to a protest can be a way to help kids who are dealing with big feelings about important issues. Protests are events where big feelings drive the action. In many cases, this can be **empowering**. In some cases, though, it can lead to violence.

Fights can sometimes break out between protesters and counterprotesters or between protesters and police officers. In some cases, protests turn into riots, which are violent public gatherings that **disturb** the peace. Many people believe kids should stay away from protests because they're not always peaceful and not always safe.

Know the Facts!

Protests take place around the world. According to Amnesty International, which is a group that fights for human rights, authorities in more than 85 countries have used unlawful force against protesters.

Protests are important, but they're not always safe. Many adults believe kids shouldn't go to protests because their safety is more important than anything they might learn at one of these events.

Using Your VOICE

For many people, safety is the most important thing to keep in mind when debating whether or not kids should go to protests. While some people argue that there's always a chance that a protest will turn violent, others argue that most protests are peaceful. They believe there's a way to show kids the power of a protest while still keeping them safe.

After learning more about protests, do you think kids should go to them? If you feel strongly about an issue and want to go to a protest, talk to a trusted adult about going to one together.

Know the Facts!

There are other ways to take action if you don't want to go to a protest. You can write a letter to a government leader, raise money to support a cause you care about, collect clothes or food for people in need, and remind adults in your life to vote.

Should kids go to protests?

YES

- Kids are old enough to face many problems in the world, so they're old enough to form their own opinions and to fight for change.
- Kids are the ones who will be in charge in the future, so they get to use their voices to say what they want the future to look like.
- Protests are a way for kids to learn about their rights and to practice active citizenship.
- Protests can help kids turn anxiety about the world into action.

NO

- Protests only show kids one side of an issue, so kids only learn what the adults around them want them to learn.
- Protests aren't usually meant for kids—they can teach kids bad words, show them bad behavior, and expose them to hate.
- Protests can be crowded and loud, which can make kids feel anxious.
- Protests are not always safe and can sometimes turn violent.

You can use a chart such as this one to help you break down important debates and decide where you stand. It's also important to use facts to support your opinions. Feelings and facts can work together!

GLOSSARY

affect: To produce an effect on something.

climate change: Change in Earth's weather over a long period of time that is caused by human activity.

debate: An argument or discussion about an issue, generally between two sides. Also, to take part in such an argument or discussion.

disturb: To make something disordered or upset.

empower: To make someone feel powerful.

expose: To make open to an action or influence.

intolerance: The state of being unwilling to accept people who are different in some way.

political: Relating to government and beliefs about how governments should work.

protect: To keep safe.

racism: The practice of treating others poorly because they are part of a different race, or group of people who look alike in certain ways. This word also relates to governments and societies that allow one race to be treated better than others.

responsibility: A duty that a person should do.

violence: The use of force to harm someone.

For More INFORMATION

WEBSITES

First Amendment: Civics 101
pbslearningmedia.org/resource/video-civics-101/first-amendment-civics-101/
This video from PBS explains the basics of the First Amendment.

KidsHealth: How Can I Worry Less?
kidshealth.org/en/kids/worry-less.html
If you worry about things that are happening in the world or things you see on the news, this article offers tips to help you cope with those worries.

BOOKS

Kaiser, Emma. *Protests*. Lake Elmo, MN: Focus Readers, 2022.

Mara, Wil. *I'm an Activist*. New York, NY: DK Publishing, 2019.

Walker, Tracy Sue. *Climate Change Activism*. Minneapolis, MN: Lerner Publications, 2023.

INDEX